Words Becoming Action

Deontae Dixon

Words Becoming Action

By Deontae Dixon © 2020

Library of Congress Control Number: 2020922762

1 John 1:1 "In the beginning was the Word of God, and the Word was with God, and the Word was God."

Table of Contents

Chapter One 1

Chapter Two 11

Chapter Three 19

Chapter Four 27

Chapter Five 35

Chapter Six 37

Chapter Seven 41

Chapter Eight 43

Chapter Nine 45

Chapter One

How can words become action?

"Watch your thoughts, they become words; watch your words, they become your actions; watch your actions, they become your habits; watch your habits, they become your character; watch your character, it becomes your destiny." – Lao Tzu

Words are very powerful. They are a strong force that is simultaneously creative and destructive. The bible records show that there was nothing created until God said three powerful words, "Let there be...."

Words have started wars and words have destroyed men, they have captured kings, they have ruined kingdoms, and they have oppressed nations. Words have birthed brilliant discoveries, and words continually sustain influence, they have reach, and they have power.

The thing about words is that there are no small, inconsequential words. Every word spoken carries potent power and they always leave either a remarkably positive effect or they'll leave a negative effect. Unfortunately, many of us do not realize the effect of the words that we speak until the negative effects that speaking negative words cause in our lives, and then as we try to understand why we have such misfortunes in our lives, we start to analyze our words.

Our actions are not a standalone factor for the results in our lives, but wanting to turnaround our actions so we can live better lives is usual useless without changing our words because our actions stem from our words, and our words stem from our thoughts.

To make any meaningful change to our lives, we must be in control of our words and our actions, and the only way to get a grip of them is by nipping them in the bud at their source point; our thoughts.

Let's think of our thoughts as we would think of fire from a match stick. On its own, the strike from a match stick is almost harmless, but once it comes in contact with fuel, it's going to start a fire, but when controlled it can be used to cook food, and if it's left uncontrolled it may burn things down. Our thoughts are fuel that can cause our words to become more pronounced and then, the actions we take to control the burning fire, or to leave it ablaze will determine the end result.

The first call for action, is for us to control our thoughts, and the best way to control our thoughts is through practicing mindfulness.

Turning our negative words into positive words through the practice of mindfulness

"Words cannot only create emotions, they create actions. And from actions flow the results of our lives." Tony Robbins

The space between our thoughts and our actions are our words. Our words give our thoughts meaning and this meaning is what we express through our actions. Every man needs to own that space between his thoughts and his words, and be in control of it through mindfulness.

We live in a very busy world and many people mistake being out and about for progress. We call it the daily hustle and bustle, and we align ourselves to grind it out even though we are literally living in chaos. We inevitably accumulate stress daily and this degenerates into conflicting thoughts that robs us of self-awareness and consciousness about our immediate environment.

Mindfulness is a practice that will take us out of the realm of chaos and transport us to a place where we'll connect to our inner self. Our inner self houses the deepest and most profound truths about us, some of which we'll be too shocked to find out. It knows all of our troubles and only it can give us the right solution for our troubles. So, we need to submit to our inner self rather than be driven wildly around by our clouded thoughts.

What practicing mindfulness will do for us is help us take charge of our thoughts and to keep them independent of the chaos around us. Mindfulness will help us to think clear and weighted thoughts that will then help us speak positive words, carry out positive actions, and then, it will positively improve our productivity and help us to live a refreshing life. Having control over our thoughts will give us the power to carefully choose our words, and to carefully map out our actions.

To practice mindfulness, we need to engage in activities that will cut us off from the chaos we are used to and help us grow in the presence of silence. Being silent is not a state that many of us are known to pursue but that is the state where our thoughts can thrive and they'll become very productive. We do not need to escape the chaos by drowning ourselves in alcohol or resorting to drugs, instead; we need to starve our distractions, reflect and imagine, while we create the pathway for positive thoughts, positive words, and positive actions that will eventually lead to positive results for our lives. The key to living our most productive life is with us, and we must take control of our lives by taking control over our thoughts and our words.

Our words become action when we speak them into existence. I contradict myself often, that's because I unconsciously allowed words without any meaning to escape my lips just bumping my gums because I was unaware of what I wanted to say. I blab instead of communicating my words precisely. In the book of Proverbs chapter 16:23, it says: "The heart of the wise makes his speech judicious and adds persuasiveness to his lips." I'm compelled to react, once that I realize that what I said wasn't wise. I feel obligated to reiterate those words because I don't want to speak negative things into existence. I begin to look for other words to articulate the conversation, I begin to rake my brain for other words to use.

    What words can I use to speak positive things into existence? "Keep the faith," "Keep holding on," "Trouble don't last always." As I grasp my faith, I come to the realization that life is not a one-hundred-yard dash, life is a marathon. I received that realization as I stand here hunched over gasping for air. I have come to a quick pit stop in my life, I had to stop to catch my breath, and now I must move on. I had to pick myself up, and I had to dust myself off. "If first you don't succeed, dust yourself off and try again, "Aaliyah. I must keep on moving until I reach the finish line. Those words became action after I took my first step back on my quest for success. On your mark, get set, ready, go!

    I must move on, and I must move at a steady pace if I plan on winning the race. I must move with an assertive attitude as I establish momentum. I must stay on the right track, in the right frame of mind, and with the right dialog. I must put my best foot forward as I proceed.

    Words become action when I stop talking about it, and I start being about it. It's time to perform, it's lights, camera, action! I have to stick to the script; I have to recite each word for word until I've learned the dialogue by heart. I have to play my part in order to advance the plot. I have to change the settings from location to location, and I have to substitute some of the characters in order to advance my story. It was suggested in several A.A. groups that we should change our play grounds, and that we should change our playmates. It was suggested that we should avoid certain areas, and it was suggested that we should avoid certain people. In the book of 1 Corinthians 15:23 it says: "Bad company ruins good morals." I find myself reverting back to those same locations that populate like-minded individuals every time that I've relapsed. I have to reside in the same type of neighborhoods each and every time that I have to start all over again. I have to properly navigate my course with a definite plan of action. That's when those playgrounds become a battlefield because I'm constantly fighting temptation. That's when I need to believe in that power greater than myself so I can resist the sudden urge to deviate from my course. That's when I need to turn my will and my life over to the care of God. That's when I need to substitute going in to those caution yellow taped areas with going to church or to a meeting, the library or to the gym; that's when I need to substitute reaching out to old friends with contacting my sponsor. I'm stepping out on faith, and I'm stepping through the battlefield waring the full armor of God.

In the book of Ephesians 6:10-19 it says; "Be strong in the Lord and in the strength of his might. Put on the whole armor of God, that you may be able to stand against the schemes of the devil. For we do not wrestle against flesh and blood, but against the rulers, against authorities, against cosmic powers over this present darkness, against the spiritual forces of evil in heavenly places. Therefore, take up the whole armor of God, that you may be able to stand in the evil day, and having done all to stand firm. Stand therefore, having fastened on the belt of truth, and having put on the readiness given by the gospel of peace. In circumstances take up the shield of faith, which you can extinguish all of the flaming darts of the evil one; and take up the helmet of salvation, and the sword of the spirit, with all prayer and supplication. To that end keep alert with all perseverance, making supplications for all the saints, and also for me, that words may be given to me in opening my mouth boldly to proclaim the mystery of the gospel.

"I'm afraid of change because it's hard to adapt, I'm afraid to fall because it's hard to bounce back." I'm Frustrated!

I had to adjust myself emotionally in order to adapt to the constant changes in my life. I have slipped in many areas in my life, and I have fell several times navigating my course. I had sat there embarrassed for a moment when I noticed people laughing at my pain, but I acquired the courage to move on. In the book of 1 Corinthians 16:13 it says: Be watchful stand firm in faith, act like Men, be strong.

I had chosen to take action steps when I realized that the reason that I had slipped and I had fell was because I am an alcoholic and an addict. I admit that I am powerless over alcohol and drugs and that my life has become unmanageable. I had taken the first step, Step One A.A. I had reclaimed my life after I spoke those words into existence, those words became action. I realized that I have a better chance at life living soberly, and I need to get sober and that I needed to remain sober in order to live proactively. I need to have a clear head so that I can handle those common disappointments that I'm going to face in life, I can handle the frustration with clarity sober minded.

I rhyme about my feelings of frustration, I rhyme about how I felt, and I wrote a book about the effects those emotions caused me. I package those two products together to be consumed by the masses of society worldwide. I'm a professional writer/composer and I'm a professional publisher/administrator. Those words became action once they were written, those words became action when they were recited over beats, those words became action once they were published. I had run across the opportunity to vent. I have the resources to change those emotions, I have the resources to perfect my character. "We will not be judge by the color of our skin but by the contents of our character." Those are wise words from the late Dr. Martin Luther King JR.

I'm Frustrated Thoughts Becoming Words is the second book that I've wrote and the first book that I've published. It's about all the disappointments that I've face throughout my life; thus far. I wrote about the discouragement that I felt when I became addicted to alcohol and drugs. I explain the discouragement that I felt as an adult because I allowed those negative thoughts, those negative emotions, and those negative words to impact my life. I showed my readers how I accepted those emotions and I show them how I moved on.

I have an active plan of action. I implemented a goal setting work sheet, there's an anger management work sheet, and there's a stress management work sheet in the back of my book. I became compelled to overcome procrastination once I followed the suggestions that are in the goal setting work sheet. I set goals, I made plans, I analyzed, and then I strategized. Those are the particular techniques and skills that I applied; those words became action once I set some realistic goals.

"Honesty is the first chapter in the book of wisdom." Wise words from the late Thomas Jefferson.

We must keep it real with ourselves before we can keep it real with someone else. Being honest with ourselves takes courage, it takes an authentic person to pin point their flaws, it takes genuine characteristics for someone to attempt to perfect their imperfections. Being honest with ourselves is the only way that we can truly know ourselves.

I can't lighten up, I have to tighten up, I have to tighten up those loose screws. I have to find it in myself to change those defects of character. I have to actively work the steps that are prescribed in order to recover. "I came to believe that a power greater than myself could restore me to sanity." It was right after that I reached Step Two of Alcoholics Anonymous that I had begun to think about my purpose driven life because I'm living on purpose. In the book of Romans 8:27-28 it says; "And he who searches hearts knows what is the mind of the spirit because the spirit intercedes for saints according to the will of God, all things work together for good, for those who are called according to his purpose."

God is all knowing, and he knows our hearts. It's about God, it's not about me. In the book of Colossians 1:16 it says; "Everything got started in him, and finds its purpose in him." God is the only power that's greater than myself that can restore me to sanity.

I embrace the word of God firmly as I take these steps towards my recovery. I believe with my heart, and I confessed with my mouth that Jesus is the way, the truth, and the light. "I made a decision to turn my will and my life over to the care of God as I understand him." Step Three of Alcoholics Anonymous.

I silently uttered those words before I took those action steps towards turning my will and my life over to the care of God. I had turned my will and my life over to the care of God by reading his word, by believing his word, and by attempting to abide by the word of God.

It's important that I take heed to the word of God, and it's necessary that I take those steps to eliminate the frustration. I can't do it by myself, I need you God! I need you every day and every step of the way! Thine will not mines be done.

"I made a searching and fearless inventory of myself." I had taken Step Four of A.A. when I wrote I'm Frustrated Thoughts Becoming Words. "I admitted to God, to myself, and to another human being the exact nature of my wrongs." I'm taking another step; I'm taking Step Five of A.A.

I thank God for renewing my thoughts, I thank God for helping me carefully select my words, and I thank you God for alleviating the frustration in my life. My life is an open book, I exposed my insecurities, I've finally realized how immature that I looked.

I have to do some house cleaning, and I have to view life with rigorous honesty. I will not continue to harbor feelings of frustrations, I will not continue to conceal feelings of discouragement, feelings of disappointment, feelings of anger, or feelings of any resentments. I've had it up to here with those emotions, those emotions were bottled up, and those emotions had surface and they became words. I used those emotions as an excuse to get high, I used those emotions as an excuse to get drunk, I used them as an excuse to act foolish, and I used them as a reason to quit.

In the book of 2 Timothy 2:20-22 it says; "Now in a great house there are not only vessels of gold and silver but also of wood and clay, some for honorable use some for dishonorable. Therefore, if anyone cleanses himself from what is dishonorable, he will be a vessel for honorable use, set apart as holy, useful to the master of the house, ready for every good work. So, flee youthful passions and pursue righteousness, faith, love, and peace, along with those who call on the lord from a pure heart.

Chapter Two

"Choosing my words wisely"

"Words can inspire. And words can destroy. Choose your words well" Robin Sharma

There is a mystery behind words that makes them so powerful. Words are not ordinary and even though they seem innocent, their effects are usually more potent than the greatest forces known to man. Every single pronouncement from your mouth matters and this was why it was important to trace how our words are formed from our thoughts, and how they lead to our actions, and the results that we eventually get.

Take a look at your life and current situation right now, are you happy with your life?

Do you know that you can make your life become more beautiful?

Do you know that you can positively turnaround your situation no matter how difficult it may seem right now?

You probably want to know how all of this could be possible for you, don't you?

The key is to unlocking all of these things and making your life to become better is through the power of your words.

By now, you are fully abreast of how your words form and the impact they have on your life, and this is why it is highly imperative for you to know how to tap into the creative force and the power in your words, by learning how to choose your words wisely.

Words Becoming Action

If you see a man who seems to be in charge of his life, he's enjoying abundance, having favorable circumstances and events happen around him, and everything just seems to be falling in place with minimal efforts; if you ask that man his secret, you shouldn't be surprised if he tells you that it's because he chooses his words wisely.

The creative power words carry is incredible and even the most powerful scientist have not been able to unravel them. Across philosophy, religion, and the deepest area of knowledge known to man, words are significantly present at the center surrounded by so much power, and for you too, your life is centered around the words that you choose. This is why you have to be intentional about them at all times.

Our world is a big magnet and this is why one of the most potent natural laws is the law of attraction. The law of attraction operates by bringing whatever you think, say, desire, or wish for, to you in multiple folds. It's more like you attaching a coin to a small ball of magnet, and then putting the small ball of magnet into a big jar containing more coins. Instead of losing your coin, your small ball of magnet will attract even more coins to you.

The law of attraction gives you more of what you already have. If what you have is negative, the law of attraction will simply give you more negative stuff to handle, but if what you have is positive, the law of attraction will give you more positive stuff.

Remember that your words are inseparable from your thoughts. What you should also remember is that the law of attraction responds to your thoughts and the words that you say, and then surrounds you with those things that you always think and say constantly.

The words you choose and speak over your life are powerful affirmations. They operate like that small ball of magnet that

Chapter Two

helps you attract more coins rather than cause you to lose the one you already have.

Surely, you would want your words to be blessings over your life and nothing else, so as we proceed, you will learn how to tap into the power of your words and you will learn how to carry them, how to know the right time to unleash them and the perfect way to use them to influence and change the course of your life positively.

Now that you know that the words that you speak carry a creative and destructive power, let's dive into using your words to create a beautiful life for yourself.

How to choose words wisely to change your life

"If we understood the power of our thoughts, we would guard them more closely. If we understood the awesome power of our words, we would prefer silence to almost anything negative. In our thoughts and words, we create our own weakness and our own strengths." Betty Eadie

The words we speak are not just vessels to convey our emotions and to express our feelings. They hold much more importance and can help us create brilliant experiences that will eventually change the dynamics surrounding our emotions and feelings.

Friend, your words can shape your destiny, and help you create the world of your dreams. It is totally possible but only when your words are "seasoned with salt." This means that your words must be true, kind, assuring, loving, confident, powerful, soothing, positive, grateful, uplifting, joyful, starting with yourself, and with everyone you meet.

If you ask someone how their doing, and they respond with a monotonous "I'm fine," or if they say, "I'm feeling great," or "I'm feeling excited," which of these is going to have a positive effect on you?

Now do you understand? This is how simple it is to use the power and the gift of words to create the world you desire. By doing this, you automatically surround yourself with wise words that will keep you and others around you abundantly strengthened, and you will be sure to get those same affirmations in multiple folds.

To begin is easy, and that is making these small changes to your thoughts, and how you interact with others around you until it becomes your normal expression.

Make it a habit to always choose words that announce happiness when you talk, and you should carve your conversations around them. How? Follow these steps that will be highlighted below:

1. Sweep through your thoughts. They are the bedrock for the words you speak and unless they are tuned right, you cannot find the right words. You should kick out negative thoughts right before their seeds settle and grow in your mind. Surround your thoughts with joy and gladness.

2. Before saying anything, pause and ask yourself the following questions:

    i. Are my words true?

    ii. Are my words necessary?

    iii. Are my words kind?

    iv. Will my words solve any problem or create more problems?

    v. Is this the right time to speak?

    vi. Will my words help me achieve a positive result?

    vii. Is silence a better option?

    viii. Will my words motivate, encourage, elevate, and uplift others will my words tear down, crush spirits, and pull others down?

    ix. If the same words were said to me, how would I feel?

3. Commit to leaving a positive impact with your words and this will happen when you begin to avoid gossips and complaints. Always focus on how to make another person better and not how to shine light on their mistakes.

4. Practice affirmations. Sow beautiful words into your life at every chance you get. These words should be the truth you want to be evident in your life, and should never be a reflection of your current situation. Be confident as you speak the words you want to sow, and believe in faith as those words manifest and produce fruit in your life.

5. When in a difficult situation, identify the things that you feel grateful for, your words will become more positive and you will begin to elevate yourself above the situation.

6. When you hear people speaking negatively, make it a habit to admonish them and to encourage them to use wise and positive words on the spot. This will train your brain to be attentive and intuitively turnaround every negative into a positive.

7. Share your good news with others. Be very excited when you hear happy stories about others.

The key to living a powerful life filled with abundance and all of your hearts desires is in the words you choose. The words you choose will always be a reflection of you, and they will determine the results that you will get. You are what you say that you are, and this is why you must safely guard the source of your words; your thoughts, as they will eventually be the story of your life.

Words become action, they set motion to your dreams, your goals, and your aspirations. Choose words that will help you grow and overcome your obstacles. Choose words that will help you see opportunities where others don't see them. Choose words that will be present in the reality that you desire. Use the magic and the power in your words to make greatness a part of your everyday essence.

As Lovasik would say, "**Kind words are a creative force, a power that concurs in the building up all that is good, and energy that showers blessings upon the world.**" Make this our motto as you choose beautiful and powerful words that will make your life and the lives of others around you shine brightly.

It was an adventure writing my first book, it was a scavenger hunt for words. I had to find the right words to convey my point of view, and I had to find the right words to express my emotions. Now I feel an urgent need to reiterate those words of frustration, and I find it necessary to control those emotions by controlling my thoughts. In the book 2 Timothy 2:14-16 it says; "Remind them of these things, and charge them before God not to quarrel about words, which does no good, but only ruins the hearers. Do you best to present yourself to God as one approved, a worker who has no need to be ashamed, rightly handling the word of truth. But avoid irreverent babble, for it will lead people into more and more ungodliness."

I had sat silently in a circle of fellow alcoholics and addicts; I had attended a mandatory six o clock meeting at the old salvation army building on 24th ${}^{St.}$ in Kansas City, MO. I was referred to the treatment facility by my P.O. after I was violated for dropping a dirty U.A. I was frustrated I didn't want to be there; I didn't think that I had a problem. I held onto reservations to drink and to use drugs once I was released as I sat there. I quietly observed the faces of the other men who were gravely impacted by the illness of alcoholism. I carefully listened to each of their stories as they shared their negative experiences with alcohol and drugs. I was at awe with some of the tales that I heard, I had pondered some of my recent encounters with alcohol and drugs as I sat there. The room was silent for a moment as I browsed it, it was my turn to share. I didn't have anything positive to say, so I passed.

Over the course of the years, I tried abstinence from alcohol and drugs, I tried quitting until I found a job, I had stopped smoking and I had stopped drinking while I was on paper. I was aware of the impact that using any controlled substances had on my life, that became apparent after relapse after relapse. I had reached Step Six of A.A. "I became entirely ready to have God remove all of those defects of character."

It was nearly over a decade that I was released from parole. I had no more obligations to the state, the only obligations that I had was to manage my own affairs without the use of any controlled substances. I had sat in an eight-o clock meeting ten years later with a burning desire to share. I had diligently searched my brain trying to find the right words to share some of my experiences. "I'm Deontae and I'm an alcoholic and an addict, I admit that I am powerless over alcohol and drugs and that my life has become unmanageable." I said before I passed.

I had quoted those words sincerely; I had quoted the first step of Alcoholics Anonymous. I needed to remind myself of that daily, I needed to repeat that over and over and over again until those words begin to sink in. I need those words to be written on my heart, and I need those words to be at the forefront of my brain. I had chosen those words because I needed to replace my frustrating thoughts and my discouraging feelings with inspiring thoughts, and encouraging feelings.

It was during the time that I completed the first draft of my second book when I begin to follow the teachings of motivational speakers. I would quietly occupy my place of residence while I listened to the gospel of the Bishop T.D. Jakes, I listened to the teachings of the Pastor Les Brown, and I had listened to the motivational speeches of Joel Osteen. I would listen to them for hours as I detoxed off of alcohol and drugs. I can't explain how good I felt after hearing their message, it was a transforming experience to me, their inspirational messages had lingered in my mind and it was renewing me. Their message wasn't anything like the typical every day jargon that I was used to, it wasn't like the everyday gangster rap that I consumed, those words of despair couldn't compare. Their message gave me alternatives to my point of view on life, while the consumption of gangster rap gave my confirmations of my feelings of strife, my lack of trust, and it also enhanced my criminality at times. I know those words by heart, I recite those words verbatim often. I'm certified and I'm qualified to spit that G-shit, but I had begun to seek another dialogue. It's important for me to choose my words wisely in my attempt to increase my level of communication.

Chapter Three
Finding better ways to express myself

I express myself by using several methods of communication, that are various ways that a person can express themselves when they use the correct words. One way that I express myself is through writing literature, I've wrote two books, thus far. Instead of glorifying the ghetto walk of life, I edify it. I can tell a story from a negative point of view, or I can show the story from a positive point of view. I have to use specific words instead of vague words to narrate the unseen and the untold stories of America's housing projects. I don't need to use big and hard to pronounce words, I need to speak everyday language that's easy for my readers to comprehend.

I have a wide range of topics to select from to narrate the unseen and the untold stories of the ghetto. I can dig deep into my imagination, and I can scribble some of the most vivid stories that someone could imagine. I observe the simplest things as a writer, it's plenty of things to write about in the ghetto. Such as; a balled up brown paper bag tumbling down the street as the wind blew, a pile of Tabaco heaped up along the curb, or a dozen of broken beer bottles that were scattered around the dumpster at the end of our block. I express my gratitude to the mothers in our community that made us sit down and eat lunch before we went outside to play, or the middle age crossing guard that help us cross the street before and after we boarded the bus for school. It's not that hard for me to express myself while I write literature.

Words Becoming Action

Another way that I can express myself is through rhythm and poetry better known as RAP. I'm a professional rhyme writer, I write rhymes to express what's on my mind. It was advised by my JR. High School teacher to write what I feel. She had told me that right before our first writing assignment, the class was instructed to write a poem.

I was in my first hour class, I was in the seventh grade, and I was only twelve years old when I joined a gang. It was long after my initiation that we lost one of our members, I was in pain, his death was unbelievable to me. It was the first time in my life that I had experienced death. I had sat in my Language Arts class with visions of his funeral running through my mind, and I had begun to write.

It wasn't too long after that that I had started to write gangster raps. I would metaphorically and lyrically express the way that I felt about the rival gang. "Pop pop, bang bang, it's all about the deuce gang," I wrote. It wasn't long after that that those words became action. I was on the front line; I was a front-line soldier. I had received stripes, and I had received rank in our neighborhood. Once those words became action, our playgrounds had turned into a battlefield.

I speak for the majority of the soldiers in our hood, and the soldiers throughout the battlefields in America, we have reached our turning point in life. It's nearly all of us, from all rags, whether it was death or jail to bring forth change. It's always warning before destruction, for many of us it took a life threating experience before most of us changed our point of view on life. Some of us have dedicated our lives to Christ after we accepted him into our hearts. Now we choose to stand united as soldiers of God's army on the battlefield's throughout America. We fight for our rights and we fight for a better life, we declare life, liberty, and a pursuit of happiness here in

America. We choose to express ourselves through advocacy, through community outreach, through volunteer work, and we express ourselves through mentorship, but most of all we express ourselves to God through prayer.

FINDING BETTER WAYS TO EXPRESS OURSELVES

Exploring better options to express ourselves and to transition our words into actions

Words are life giving. They can turn around a negative situation into a brilliant experience. In the last two chapters that I shared with you, I have explained how we form our words and the effects they have on us when we speak them. I however need to let you know that the extent of the experience that your words can create for you depends on the power in the kind of words that you use.

I'll show you what I mean in this chapter. Please follow closely.

You see, your thoughts, feelings, and emotions need words to fully come alive. This is why you need to constantly find ways to push and turn them into actions. This is why the key to getting the best out of your life in any situation lies in finding words that fully expresses the depth and extent of all of your thoughts, feelings, and emotions.

Words carry different weights, but one big disservice that you can do to yourself is using words that do not capture the true state of what you feel. When the words you speak do not match the intensity of your thoughts, feelings, and emotions, there will be a disconnect and this will not help you create the changes you actually desire or deserve.

The importance of finding better ways to express yourself is connected to effecting the changes that you desire in your life, but this can only be achievable if you know how to use words to make your situation better. Once you know how to better express yourself with words, you can then rely on your thoughts to help you get the best out of your life. Once you unlock better ways to express yourself, you will realize that there will not be any limitations to bringing your biggest imaginations to life once you can fully express your thoughts through your words.

You can find better ways to express yourself, but first, you have to breakdown your belief systems.

BREAKING DOWN THE PILLARS OF OUR BELIEF SYSTEMS

You and I are a product of our belief system and the patterns that we have formed over time. In many instances, the things that we know may not be 100% true but once we hold it dear to our hearts, they become ideas that will be reinforced overtime.

These belief patterns also have effects on how you use our words to express ourselves and they determine who we are. The steps to making changes and finding better expressions for ourselves begins with us deliberately going against the flow of the moving waters that we have been used to. We must come out of the safety pockets that we have used to define ourselves and we need to break out of familiar grounds. As we do this, we'll be faced with the fear of the unknown and this will likely keep us grounded in the same spot.

Changes will cost us and this is why we cannot remain in a dead end because it feels comfortable when there is more out there for us, we must take the plunge.

Once we are determined to go against those beliefs that we have been used to in the past, it becomes very easy for you to find better ways to express ourselves.

Chapter Three

WHAT WE MUST DO TO FIND BETTER WAYS TO EXPRESS OURSELVES

Finding better ways to express ourselves is a challenge that we must take on for ourselves. It's through this that we'll be able to unlock better ways to transition our conversations.

What we need to do to find better ways to express ourselves is captured in the following points:

- Be conversant and fully aware of the choices before us and take charge.
- Do not shy away from exerting our authority over our lives.
- Make decisions based around our choices.
- Change doesn't happen in an instant so, we must gradually take on change by making small but effective adjustments.
- Encourage others to change too by teaching them to take actions that exerts their authority over their lives; not your authority or any other person's authority.
- Listen more and dwell on our thoughts; learn from our thoughts and map out possible actions that will drive meaningful change to our lives. We must also reflect on these thoughts and actions with an open and committed mind to giving our lives more value.
- Give our feelings more meaning by making efforts to capture every feeling and connecting them to a tangible aspect of our lives, especially something that we can see physically.

- Internalize new information and fully embrace the new perspectives and fresh insights that we get from our thoughts to give us a better understanding.
- Always tap into everything that inspires us and make sure we do something with the inspiration.

TRANSITIONING OUR WORDS EFFECTIVELY INTO ACTIONS THROUGH BETTER MEANS OF EXPRESSION

Learning to transition our words into actions requires a great deal of commitment from all of us. Transitioning our words effectively doesn't happen like magic, it happens by staying conscious of the things that we're attempting to convey.

A little bit of work is necessary for change to happen, but we cannot begin to work without understanding why we have to do the work. The question that we should always ask ourselves is, what will I get from finding a better way to express myself? Our answer should be the motivation that we need to drive us to escape our current frame of mind. We have to hold this answer very dear to our hearts. This answer should help us to change our mindset, give us the inspiration to embrace positivity, and it should give us perspective that will make the actions follow without even realizing it.

Properly transitioned words will produce beautiful results for our lives.

Here are some things that we can do to transition our words more effectively.

- Use Body Language – body language helps you to combine action with your words. Combining words and actions helps to capture the full extent of the meaning you are looking to convey, and it allows us to accurately describe our subconscious through the motion of our body. Speaking effectively has to do more with carefully communicating our mind and not just having a hold on the physical.

- Be mindful of emotions – our emotions can either run high or they can run low, and they can affect our ability to express ourselves. When our emotions are high or if they're low, our thoughts will not be processed clearly, and our communication may be off the point. What we should do is take control of our emotions by being calm and pondering more on our inner voices. We should notice all of our feelings but don't allow them to distract us from our point of view.

- Gather our thoughts before speaking – communication is not just about speaking, but it is more about understanding the purpose of why. At every point, we must think about the reason behind the conversation. What we want to achieve from the conversation should be the most important question that we should ask ourselves before speaking.

- Be assertive – when we speak, we should focus on the things that we want share. Don't stray from the immediate topic.

- Communicate clearly and respectfully – once we sense some misunderstanding, we must take it upon ourselves to clear it up so that the other party will not become defensive. Be clear, direct, and polite.

- Communicate to understand – communication without empathy is dictatorship so, your words should be directed at understanding the situation of others. Don't push your point of view down other people's throats, but instead; listen to them first, and then set compromises.

- Practice, make mistakes, learn, and practice again.

Finding better ways to express ourselves is important, it's extremely necessary to increase our growth to all aspects of our life.

Chapter Four
Speaking positive things into existence

As a kid, we were all convinced that when we do not knock-on wood, something that we said will happen. We have all been there, and this little belief that always takes us on a guilt trip during our childhood only proves that we are subconsciously aware of what words can do. Simple words can enforce a certain feeling on someone or yourself, and when not chosen wisely, it can damage someone very badly. Words are simple and necessary, but when they are chosen perfectly and delivered at the right time, they can spark hope and encourage actions.

Our world today is created from the clamor of the oppressed; from classic literatures such as Beowulf that taught us to live brave and with honor, to Anne Frank's enlightening personal accounts from the second world that made us see the horror of war, human hatred, and injustice, to today's modern-day activists who continue to create awareness on important social issues that does not seem to end. All of these have changed the world by revealing what is true and what must be changed through convincing and powerful words.

Politicians are most well-known for their convincing skills. They use and arrange words to display hope and promise to people, which in turn, help them win. They make compelling remarks and use attractive words to mold their voters' minds, until their words finally become reality as their supporters vote.

Their persuasion has become actions because it sparked hope for people and made them realize that change will soon arrive.

And as Brian Sooy, founder and Design Director of Aspire would put it, "Words help leaders cast vision for the promise of the future. Words give life to ideas. Words and phrases convey the purpose, values, character, and culture of your organization. Words that motivate create affinity and loyalty when the values conveyed are shared by those who believe in your cause."

Encouraging actions, the most commonplace for encouragement are motivational quotes; people who have felt let down turn to reading motivational quotes from famous people to feel better. But what is it that these quotes have that it gives motivation to most people and even last for generations? According to Jonathan Fader of Union Square Practice in New York, "the appeal appears to lie in a combination of good wordsmithing, motivational psychology, and a measure of self-selection. People who tend to feel inspired by motivational quotes are going to find them more resonant than those who don't find simple phrases and sayings to be particularly meaningful."

Words motivate when they are made to, but when they're not, it takes a few people with inspired hearts to see the goodness and motivation in them. It is an important skill that you know how to make simple words motivational because it's what makes people move, it's what turn words into actions. Turning words into action Words are only words when they are heard by the few, but when heard by many, it will inspire and incite action. But how do we emerge from being inhibited to becoming an outspoken, persuasive speakers?

Taken inspiration from the good book, Art of War by Sun Tzu, here are some guides that might help you choose your words in order to influence actions:

Choose your battles. A person who knows when to speak and when not to speak sends more message than a fool whose mouth is always open. Either debating with someone, or encouraging others or yourself, sometimes the perfect word to use is nothing. Silence is as powerful as the perfect word, because it means that you are acknowledging that some things are helpless, that sometimes doing nothing is the perfect action.

Timing is essential It is important that you take your time in deciding to put out the words in your mouth. Words are powerful, but only effective when used in the right scenario. If you think of it, there are phrases in life that does not make sense in a normal day, but when the time comes that you needed to hear it the most, those phrases will then only make sense at that time. Words are delicate and fragile; they should not be thrown out easily. Instead, words are supposed to be delivered delicately at the right moment when its impact is most powerful, only then that it ignites a person's will to move and take action.

Know yourself It is important to know your voice and what makes you, because words are most effective when they sound natural. In choosing the perfect words to inspire movement, you must be true to yourself and be natural. People do not like to hear words that does not feel like they come from the heart, even yourself, you know when you're just faking it and therefore you won't be able to change your mind if you're just forcing something onto you. People are smart, and they know what is real or not.

Have a unique plan Blatant motivation does not work anymore, people do not want to hear someone telling them what to do and how to do things including yourself. It's hard to impart knowledge to someone whose mind is already made up, and if our goal is to turn words into actions, then it is important to be more creative. Set yourself as an example, don't just tell yourself that you are going to do something, but rather, tell yourself what will happen if you do or do not do the action. It's like setting an ultimatum with yourself, it's always healthy to know where your actions will take you and why it is important to happen.

Disguise your plan Even when you're still far from your goal, you must use your words to remind you that you're only a few steps away. Sometimes, a little bit of deception will help a lot. An action takes a lot of work, and words are not enough to keep you going. It is important you make sure you are able to keep going, because once you stop speaking, once you stop writing, it will be harder to get back and you will eventually lose your words and that will only result to failure.

Knowing the weak and strong points Knowing what buttons to push can easily help you make a person follow or leave. Encouraging some action to someone or yourself can be hard, and it must be looked at as a challenge. Knowing the words that will motivate them or yourself is very necessary in expecting movement. You must know that not all words can make everyone move.

Change represent opportunity When words turn bitter, you can always add sugar to make it sweet. There are times that when you hear the same thing over and over again, it's hard to keep it going. Variety will always spice things up, and when even when they convey the same message, choosing different words would make it seem new. With that, it will most definitely encourage you or someone else to move and take action.

Success breeds success Knowing that there is an end game, will only lead to more reached goals. It is important that in every action you are making, you are aware of what you are going to achieve in the end. In reality, motivations only work when people see its effects happen, maybe to them or to other people. Results are the most important evidence that something is or is not achieved at the end.

Chapter Four

No one profits from prolonged warfare Words only annoy when they are repeatedly thrown at you. Imagine repeating a word over and over for days, not only that it will annoy you, but you will eventually get sick of that particular word and probably you won't want to hear it ever again. It's the same with motivational talks or pep talks, you will not be able influence if you use the same thing every time. You will know when it's ran its course, you'll know when to change, because you, yourself, will eventually get tired of it. At the end of the end, the only thing that will push you and other people is your willingness and consistency; willingness to do, and consistency in using words to drive you into action.

Remember that words become actions. They become a catalyst to a greater purpose once you have learned how to use them properly. Embrace that power, that skill, because maybe then you can change the world.

Claim it and then go obtain it

Whenever I claim anything that I want, I believe it with all of my heart that it's mines. I honestly believe that it belongs to me. I'm speaking it into existence without a shadow of a doubt. I'm owning that, I'm laying claim on it. I'm committed to achieve my goals because my mind and my heart has conceived it, I can acquire whatever my heart desires, what the mind can conceive and believe the mind can achieve.

Having Faith

I can speak on it until I turn purple in the face, and I can talk about it until my mouth gets dry, but if I don't take action, if I don't put in the work to acquire it, there's a good chance that I won't get it if I'm not committed.

In the book of proverbs 14:23 "In all toil there is profit but mere talk only tends to poverty."

It's not just going to fall out of the sky and land in my lap, it doesn't matter how much I believe that I deserve it, I have to earn it. I can't succeed if I don't try. If I have faith, it's a better chance that I won't give up until I get it, but I have to be a go getter.

Being Confident

You have to possess the self-confidence to go after it, and your heart has to be in it. You've claimed it with confidence; therefore, you're speaking it into existence. You've confidently converted words into action when you speak them with confidence.

Believe in yourself

"Believe in yourself," those words become action because you believe that you got what it takes to get whatever you want. It doesn't matter what it is, it doesn't matter if it's a certain amount of money, it doesn't matter if it's a new career, it doesn't matter if it's an expensive automobile, or if it's a new house. A person must believe that they're capable of having what they desire. We have to believe that we deserve it. We have to know without doubt that it's ours because we believe in ourselves, and first and foremost, we believe in God.

Be specific

I have a realistic perception of how I plan to acquire whatever I want. It doesn't matter what it is, I can obtain it if I'm specific. I've already claimed it, and I'm taking action steps towards obtaining it. I have faith, I'm faithfully committed in order to receive it. I'm confident that it's mines because I believe that I have what it takes to get it. It's attainable because I 've pinpointed what I want.

Having vision

I have vision because I've perceived it, and I've conceived it. I've visualized it, I've imagined myself with it, now I can see myself possessing what I want.

Staying focused

Now that I'm specific about what I want, now that I can see myself acquiring it, now that I have vision, I have to stay focused on getting it. I've located it, I know exactly how much it cost, I've figured out everything that I need to do to achieve it, but I can't lose focus. It's attainable, it's within my grasp, but I can't lose sight of it. I have to keep my eyes on the prize.

Having goals

Once I've pin pointed my target, I have to stay on point like an arrow if I plan on hitting the bull's eye. I have to stay focused on my mark once I set goals. I have set immediate goals, I have set short term goals, and I have set long term goals. It depends on whatever it is that I claim that I want, and it depends on how much time and money that I'm willing to invest on accomplishing my goals. I turned words into action once I have set clearly defined goals.

Chapter Five
Be a man of your word

Liars are untrustworthy individuals because they don't keep their word, their word doesn't have value once they're caught in a lie because I can't believe what they say. If you lie to me then you'll steal from me. Liars are unreliable, they are not dependable people. Words become action once we believe them, lies become action because they give birth to more lies.

When a man is sincerely about his word, he's committed to showing you that what he has told you is the truth. He can show you by his actions, and not through his words. A man about his word is a committed and dedicated man, he's a faithful and he's an honest man. A man about his word stays the course, he doesn't deviate. He's steadfast and unmovable because he's grounded in truth. Being about your word only takes a small effort, it's not hard to be honest, it's not hard to be genuine. When a man is genuine, he's committed to whatever it is that he's involved in, and he follows through. He keeps his promises, he doesn't breach contracts, or nor does he break agreements. He accepts the bitter with the sweet, he's willing to enjoy the good times, and he endures the bad times. He doesn't leave when the going gets tough, he's there when the sun shines, and he's there when it rains, he's not a fair-weather man. A man about his word usually arrives early and he usually leaves late because he's committed whole heartedly.

Words Becoming Action

Be a man of your word, be prompt, be on time, and every time. A man about his word pays his debts on time, and he gives back what he borrows. A man about his word promptly admits whenever he's wrong. Be a dependable man; whenever people depend on what you say, they're believing in you, they're counting on you to follow through. Words become action when a man is about his word, words become action when a man does whatever he says he's going to do.

Being a dependable person establishes trust, it builds integrity, and it builds healthy relationships. Those are good characteristics to have, those action words are displayed they're not spoken. Those words become action because a person is held liable whenever they agree to something. It's a chain reaction whenever someone doesn't keep their word because people are depending on them, they're waiting on them to show up because they're liable.

"I humbly ask God to remove my short comings," Step Seven of A.A.

Chapter Six

My word is my bond

"I made a list of all the persons that I harmed and I became willing to make amends to them all." Step Eight of A.A.

I made a list of all the people that I've harmed, some of them were hurt by what I said, and some of them were hurt by what I done to them. The first person on that list is my Grandmother. I disregarded the bond that I had with her by being disobedient. Words cannot express the bond that I had with my Grandmother, it's an unbreakable bond because it's a spiritual bond. Her wise words were distorted by the clouds of marijuana smoke, I would attempt to drain her voice out my head with large gulps of alcohol. I wasn't completely receptive whenever she tried to bond with me, and I wasn't teachable when she attempted to pass along her infinite wisdom.

I became a full fledge alcoholic and addict when I choose to go in my own direction in life. I decide to head in the wrong direction instead of following her lead into the right direction, and I know that that hurt my Grandmother because she only wanted the best for me.

I didn't allow her words to manifest, and I now realize that's where I ran into the majority of the problems that I've faced in life, thus far. She had always told me to stay prayed up, and to always put God first. It was an entire book of the basic instructions that she directed me to. She had given me tons of advice before I left the nest to run the streets.

I ripped and I ran the streets, the streets never could run me, and they never will because I abide by the rules of the game. I have common sense, and I have good intentions. I've always thought logically enough to do the wrong thing the right way, and I've always done the right thing by people because I was raised the right way.

In the book of Galatians 6:9 it says, "And let us not grow weary while doing good, for in due season we shall reap if we do not lose heart." In the book of 2 Thessalonians 3:13 it also advises us to continue to do good, it says; "But as for you, brethren, do not grow weary, in doing good.

It was shortly after my Grandmother had passed through the gates of Heaven, and it was when I started to read the bible after several life changing experiences that I finally understood her wise words. I choose to make amends to God through Jesus Christ, and I thank you Jesus for your sacrifice for my sins.

"We made direct amends to such people whenever possible, except when to do so would injure them or others." Step Nine of A.A. This step calls for action, it requires us to take action steps towards repairing relationships after we've broken our bond with most of the people we have hurt in our addictions.

Words become action whenever we're sincere in our approach, we must be sincere whenever we request a person's forgiveness for the things that we have done to them, or for the profane things that we have said to them while we were under the influence of a control substance. I've said a lot of negative things, and I've spoken a lot of negative things into existence while I was under the influence. I had lacked self-control, I was being driven by negative emotions, such as; frustration, anger, and resentments. I've hurt a lot of people under the influence of mood-altering substances; such as, alcohol and drugs.

Chapter Six

In the book of James 3:5-10 it says; "So also the tongue is a small member, yet it boasts of great things. How great a forest is set ablaze by such a small fire! And the tongue is a fire, a world of unrighteousness. The tongue is set among our members, staining the whole body, setting on fire the entire course of life, and set on fire by hell. For every kind of beast and bird of reptile and sea creature, can be tamed and has been tamed by mankind, but no human being can tame the tongue. It is a restless evil, full of deadly poison. With it we bless our Lord and Father, and with it we curse people who are made in the likeness of God. From the same mouth came blessing and cursing. My brothers, these things ought not to be so.

It was typical for me to wake up the next day reaching out to God asking for forgiveness, and vowing to never drink or use drugs again. Then I would reach out to the woman in my life at that moment asking her for her forgiveness for my behavior. I've had to reach out to my family and my friends after a horrible evening under the influence. I've woke up in jails, and I've woke up in hospitals. I've been held responsible for hospital bills, I'm responsible for having to attend court dates, and I'm obligated to pay fines. In some occasions; I couldn't make amends directly, our differences had to be settled in the court of law.

I've burned a lot of bridges and I've broken a lot of bonds. I was able to repair some of those bridges, and I was able to mend some of those bonds because they were reconciled through Christ, but some of those bridges, I can't look back. There's a lot of people who have been offended, harmed, or hurt by what I've said or done to them. I have to have the courage to move forward, and I must possess the knowledge to understand why I cannot look back, and I have to have the compassion to respect the feelings of others.

In the book of James 3:13-18 it says; "Who is wise and understanding among you? By his good conduct let him show his works in the meekness of wisdom. But if you have bitter jealousy and selfish ambitions in your hearts, do not boast and be false to the truth. This is not the wisdom that comes from above, but it's earthly, unspiritual, demonic. For where jealousy and selfish ambition exist, there will be disorder in every vile practice. But the wisdom from above is first pure, then peaceable, gentle, open to reason, full of mercy and good fruits, impartial and sincere. And a harvest of righteousness is sown in peace by those who make peace.

"We continued to take personal inventory and when we were wrong, we promptly admitted it." Step Ten of Alcoholics Anonymous.

Step Ten of A.A. suggest that we should admit it whenever we're wrong in order to pin point our flaws in life, so we can perfect our character. I prefer to admit my wrong doing to God first, and to seek his guidance before I seek the opinion of others. I have to promptly pin point my flaws after taking inventory of my thoughts, words, and actions with discernment before I engage in a heart-to-heart conversation with another human being.

Chapter Seven
Constructive words

1 Thessalonians 4:18 "Therefore comfort one another with these words."

Most of us take it personal whenever anyone on the outside looking in takes notice of our character defects. We don't like it when people point out what they see inside of us that we need to perfect our character. It's not easy to accept their criticism because we think that we have it all figured out, we think that we have been doing good enough. We allow our pride to get in the way, and that makes us stagnant in our growth. I learned to start accepting the constructive criticism of others that have been where I'm trying to go in life, I had to learn the hard way after several failed attempts at sobriety. Constructive criticism makes us humble.

I'm a work in progress, and I'm actively seeking through prayer and meditation to improve my conscious contact with God as I understand him praying only for knowledge of his will for me and the power to carry that out. Step Eleven of A.A. are action words that inspire me to build a better relationship with God.

Every thought, every word, and every deed are seeds, and I need to plant good seeds by cultivating words of encouragement. I need to create phrases that help me build my character, I need to formulate words that increase my self-esteem whenever I say them.

In the book of Proverbs 4:20-27 it says; "My son, be attentive to my words; incline your ears to my sayings. Let them not escape your sight, keep them within your heart. For they are life to those who find them, and healing to all flesh. Keep your heart with all vigilance, for from it flows the spring of life. Put away from crooked speech, and put devious talk far from you. Let your eyes look directly forward, and your gaze be straight before you. Ponder the path of your feet, then all your ways will be sure. Do not swerve to the right or to the left, turn your feet away from evil."

"Having had a spiritual awakening as a result of these steps, we tried to carry this message to alcoholics, and to practice these principles in all our affairs." Step Twelve of A.A. encourages us to carry the message to other alcoholics, and the bible encourages us to carry the word of Christ to other believers.

I'm leaning on the word of God; I'm inspired by multiple scriptures that comfort me and that guide me whenever I'm faced with those challenges in life. The word of God helps me to redirect my focus, it puts me back in the right frame of mind.

Chapter Eight
It's not what you say, it's how you say it

I value my freedom as a Black Man, I have a right to unlimited freedom here in America. I have a right to freedom of speech, I have a right to suffrage, I have a right to free enterprise, and I have a right to equality. I have an undeniable number of rights under the U.S. Constitution, and I'm speaking loudly with clarity for those rights. I'm claiming those rights with confidence using the voice of my people as one nation under God, indivisible, with liberty and justice for all. No Justice, No Peace.

    The summer had come to an abrupt end, it was the beginning of fall in 2010. I had worked all of my sales territory on one mild fall evening, my mind wandered as I drove along my route. I was brought back to reality by the sight of a customer that had stood at the edge of the curb. It was an attractive sister that had stood about five five with a small waste and thick thighs. She had stood there with her daughter as I pulled up. I pulled to the edge of the curb and I had admired her for a moment before I had taken her order.

    "The world wasn't ready for that," I said as I browsed her from the wasted up to her face.

    "What's that?" She said with a smile on her face before she grabbed her ice cream.

    I said, "Our first black President, Hun."

    She nodded her head in agreement before she said, "Yes."

    "I stood in a mile-long line to see Barack," I said.

She had chuckled before she said, "I work for Freedom, we're working the preliminary campaign, we're working to get him re-elected."

I already had previous experience working in a call center environment raising funds for the VFW, and the RNC for Mitt Romney and Michael Huckabee back in 2008. She had raised my curiosity, and I was interested.

"How can I get involved?" I asked her.

She had directed me to the Gates BBQ shopping plaza on 12th & Brooklyn to apply for Freedom Inc. I had applied the very next day, and I had started canvassing door to door for the preliminary campaign in 2010 for President Barack Obama, Congressman Emanuel Cleaver, and Senator Robin Carnahan the day after that.

I quietly sat there and I tried to figure out various ways to convey the message to pursue potential voters to register to vote. I tried to figure out how to express the importance of voting to the people in the Black Community as I canvassed. That's when I realized that it's not what you say, it's how you say it. Those words became action with each person that I had the opportunity to connect with. Those words became action once they registered with each individual that I had the chance to talk to about the importance of voting in the Black community. I had the opportunity to connect with various walks of life throughout each community that we had canvassed. I had created a simple dialog to communicate the message of Freedom Inc. while I handed out political literature. I also stressed the importance of the U.S. Census, "We have to take a stand and get counted for a piece."

In the book of Exodus 30:12 it says; "When you take a census of the people of Israel, then each shall give a ransom for his life to the Lord when you number them, that there be no plague among them when you number them."

Chapter Nine
Say what you mean, and mean what you say

Some people blab without any point of view, they speak words without any meaning because they're unaware of what they want to say. Whenever someone is beating around the bush just bumping their gums it sounds like an inconsistent chatter. Whenever we engage in a conversation, we want our words to cause reaction because we're attempting to make a connection with whoever we're talking to. It could be a positive reaction resulting in laughter or a joyous response, or it could be a negative reaction leading to frowns and angry comments.

We need our words to have meaning, words can only become action if they're meaningful, our words must make sense. In order for our words to make sense we have to think before we speak. The most effective way to communicate our words properly is if we think before we speak. If a person has thought about what he or she is going to say to make a connection with who they're trying to reach, they'll have a better a chance for their words to register with the individual that they're communicating with if their words are well thought out. We must always think before we speak if we really want to say what we mean. Whenever we think before we speak, we know exactly what we're trying to say because we have thought it out with clarity.

Words cannot become action if people don't know what we're saying, know what I'm saying? We should always speak loudly and we should speak clearly whenever we mean what we say, we have to speak loudly and speak clearly when we're relaying an important message, words become action when they're spoken correctly. The only way that we can capitalize off our conversation is if people know exactly what we're saying, know what I'm saying?

When we are saying what we mean, making eye contact is important. When we make eye contact with whoever we are talking to, that lets them know that we're sincere about what we're saying. Making eye contact is essential to any conversation because we tend to believe an individual when we see eye to eye with them. Making eye contact expresses a person's sincerity when they're seriously trying to get, they're point across. We want people to take us seriously, we want them to ponder our words, and we want them to take our words into consideration. Whenever we say what we mean, and mean what we say our words become action, and our words are the right words they could cause the right reaction when people are listening to what we are saying.

WORDS BECOMING ACTION BY DIRTY DOLLARS © 2020

www.ingramcontent.com/pod-product-compliance
Lightning Source LLC
Chambersburg PA
CBHW050448010526
44118CB00013B/1741